# DARE
# U2 OPEN
# THIS
# BOOK

D1124781

CAROL McADAMS MOORE

# DARE U2 OPEN THIS BOOK

DRAW IT,
WRITE IT,
DARE 2 LIVE IT

**90**
DEVOTIONS

ZONDERKIDZ

*Dare U 2 Open This Book*
Copyright © 2014 by Carol Lynn Moore

Requests for information should be addressed to:

Zonderkidz, 3900 Sparks Dr. SE, Grand Rapids, Michigan 49546

ISBN 978-0-310-74297-5

Published in association with the Books & Such Literary Agency, 52 Mission Circle, Suite 122, PMB 170, Santa Rosa, CA 95409-5370, www.booksandsuch.biz.

*Cover design: Deborah Washburn*
*Interior design: David Conn*
*Interior images: Shutterstock, www.istockphoto.com*

*Printed in the United States of America*

14 15 16 17 18 19 20 /DCI/ 22 21 20 19 18 17 16 15 14 13 12 11 10 9 8 7 6 5 4 3 2 1

# ENTER HERE

Read something awesome about God.
Learn something cool about yourself. Then ...

**DOODLE**

**GLUE**

**WRITE**

**PAINT**

**SCRATCH**

Take clues from the page or just
have at it. It's fun. It's cool. It's U!

*Sweet!* Learning to follow Jesus.

**Best. Idea. Ever.**

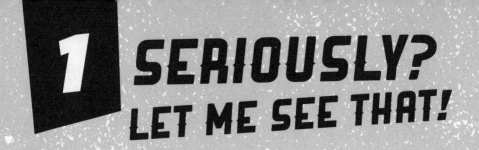

# 1 SERIOUSLY?
## LET ME SEE THAT!

*The king said to Daniel, "Surely your God is the God of gods and the Lord of kings and a revealer of mysteries, for you were able to reveal this mystery."*

Daniel 2:47

King Nebuchadnezzar had a dream, but no one could interpret it for him. Daniel prayed to the almighty God. God explained the dream to Daniel. Mystery solved!

Read all about God's power over the mysteries in Daniel 2.

Any questions 4 God about your life?

# What if . . .
you trust God to guide you in a mystery?

Think *impossible to understand*— except for you and God.
Ever wonder about things?

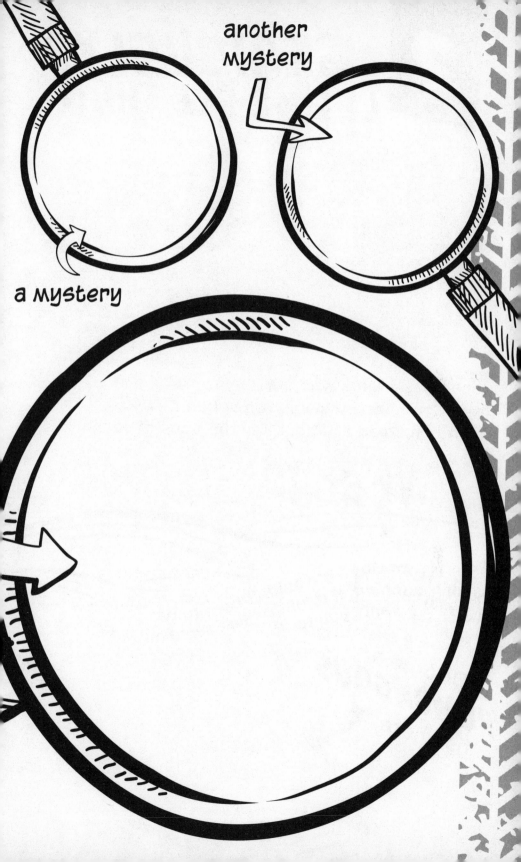

another
mystery

a mystery

# 2 SERIOUSLY?
## LET ME SEE THAT!

*Now the LORD provided a huge fish to swallow Jonah, and Jonah was in the belly of the fish three days and three nights. From inside the fish Jonah prayed to the Lord his God ... And the LORD commanded the fish, and it vomited Jonah onto dry land.*

*Jonah 1:17 – 2:1, 10*

Jonah was a dude who ran from God ... and became fish vomit. **YUCK!** Uh-huh. Read all about it in the book of Jonah.

# What if ...

you ran from God? It wouldn't have to be like real running. It might be just avoiding what he wants you to do.

Doodle a **HUMONGOUS** fish here. ↘

Wait! U are in the pic too!
   Make a list. Where would you go or what would you do to avoid God?

Me avoiding God | Me as fish vomit

How do you think God would get your attention?

# 3 SERIOUSLY?
## LET ME SEE THAT!

> For all have sinned and fall short of the glory of God, and all are justified freely by his grace through the redemption that came by Christ Jesus.
>
> Romans 3:23–24

**Guess what.**
**Nobody is perfect.**

## NONE. NADA. ZILCH. NO ONE!

But the Bible says that we can ask Jesus to forgive our sins. Ever mess up? Ever felt like *aww snap*? With Jesus—your sins can be gone. Just like that. Just ask him.

# What if ...

| you do not accept Jesus? | you do accept Jesus? |
| --- | --- |

Color this side with black crayon—**HEAVY**. Use the end of a paper clip to scratch the word **SIN**.

Write **GOD'S GRACE** on this side. Use glue.

*Okay. Finish page. Skip to tomorrow. It's cool.*

# 4 SERIOUSLY?
## LET ME SEE THAT!

**KNOW THIS**

For God so loved the world that he gave his one and only Son, that whoever believes in him shall not perish but have eternal life.

John 3:16

# What if . . .

U made Jesus your Savior and remembered John 3:16 forever? **WRITE IT HERE**

- ☐ underline it
- ☐ highlight it
- ☐ make arrows pointing to it
- ☐ put stars around it
- ☐ circle it
- ☐ say it out loud — no lookin'
- ☐ bend the page corners
- ☐ paper clip the page
- ☐ mark page — use large rubber band

## How does that happen exactly?

Just pray three things:

1. Fess up that you are a sinner.

2. Say that you understand that Jesus died for you.

3. Accept Jesus as your Lord and Savior.

**5**

## LISTEN UP!

# SERIOUSLY?
## LET ME SEE THAT!

*His face shone like the sun, and his clothes became as white as the light. ...and a voice from the cloud said, "This is my Son, whom I love; with him I am well pleased. Listen to him!"*

*Matthew 17:2, 5*

Jesus went up a mountain with some of the disciples. Suddenly he changed (think glowing like the sun) and Moses and Elijah were standing with him. Wanna know more?

## Check out Matthew 17:1–8.

# What if ...

you were on the mountain with Jesus that day? How do you think he looked? Doodle it all here. Add God's voice.

Make the edges of the page bright too. Think brighter than you have ever seen.

Dear God,

I'm gonna listen to Jesus, your Son. Here is how:

Amen

**START**

# SERIOUSLY?
## LET ME SEE THAT!

*You have searched me, Lord, and you know me. Before a word is on my tongue you, Lord, know it completely.*

*Psalm 139:1, 4*

Uh-huh. God knows everything. No joke. So R U honoring him with your thoughts and talk?

**Read Psalm 139:1–4 to see what else.**

□ my words please God

□ workin' on my words

□ my words could be better

# words out here

# What if ...

your thoughts and words honored God? Erase. Change. Fix the things you need to. Do it.
   Here is your brain. Find your way out of the maze.

What ideas are bouncing around in there? What words make it out?

# SERIOUSLY?
## LET ME SEE THAT!

**GAME PLAN**

> *"For I know the plans I have for you," declares the Lord, "plans to prosper you and not to harm you, plans to give you hope and a future."*
>
> *Jeremiah 29:11*

God used Jeremiah to write a letter to the leaders of his people. God wanted them to know for sure that he had a good plan for their future. Read ALL about it here— **Jeremiah 29:1–23!**

## What if . . .

God drew out a game plan for your life? How might it look?

Doodle the next play 4 U right now. Cut. Fold small.
Place in pocket. Live it.

**8**

# SERIOUSLY?
## LET ME SEE THAT!

**PRAISE JAM**

*Shout for joy to the LORD, all the earth, burst into jubilant song with music; make music to the LORD with the harp, with the harp and the sound of singing, with trumpets and the blast of the ram's horn — shout for joy before the LORD, the King.*

Psalm 98:4–6

There are lots of praise jams in the Bible. This one has the harp, trumpets, and the ram's horn. Set up a praise jam for the Lord on the stage.

# What if ...

Let the rivers clap their hands, let the mountains sing together for joy.

Psalm 98:8

the rivers joined in with clapping and the mountains broke out in songs of joy?
Hey! It could happen!
We're talkin' God's power here.

Add some clapping rivers and singing mountains to the praise jam.

# 9

# SERIOUSLY? LET ME SEE THAT!

*"See, I have refined you, though not as silver; I have tested you in the furnace of affliction."*

Isaiah 48:10

People use fire to melt down silver and to get all the junk out of it. The Bible talks about silver and Y-O-U. It says that you are made better by affliction (think *problems*). When you live through problems, you become a better, stronger person for Christ. It gets all the junk out of your life.

# What if . . .

you have an affliction (problem)? The truth? Everyone has some kind of affliction.

## Pop Quiz

### What's testing you?

a. a sickness

b. a bully

c. a problem at home

d. a tough time with school

e. a parent who is gone

f. an injured pet

g. none of the above

h. all of the above

Doodle an affliction you have and what God can do with it.

# SERIOUSLY?
## LET ME SEE THAT!

*In the beginning you laid the foundations of the earth, and the heavens are the work of your hands.*

*Psalm 102:25*

Look around at the earth. Love it. Look up at the skies. AWESOME! God made them.

# What if ...

you think about the most unbelievable place you have seen? The Lord, your God, made it! Where is that place? **(circle one)**

desert

ocean

forest

mountains

Doodle it here.

Now doodle more of God's amazing earth around this page. Fill it up!

Dear God,
The "work of your hands" is amazing.
The _____ is my fave because
_____. Thanks for
making such a great world for us to live in.
Amen

# 11

## SERIOUSLY?
## LET ME SEE THAT!

*Still other seed fell on good soil, where it produced a crop—a hundred, sixty or thirty times what was sown.*

Matthew 13:8

Guess what? God thinks you're dirt.

# D-I-R-T

It says it right in the Bible. The only question is *what kind* of dirt are you?

Read about ALL KINDS of dirt here: Matthew 13:1—23!

# What if ...

you are the best dirt you can be?
1. Glue a pic of you here.
2. Rub dirt on the pic.
3. Use the best dirt you can find.

Now rub more of the good dirt around the edges of this page. What might grow in the future?

# 12

# SERIOUSLY?
## LET ME SEE THAT!

*Then he [Peter] began to call down curses, and he swore to them, "I don't know the man!"*
*Immediately a rooster crowed. Then Peter remembered the word Jesus had spoken: "Before the rooster crows, you will disown me three times." And he went outside and wept bitterly.*

Matthew 26:74–75

**Jesus said that Peter would deny him three times before the rooster crowed (before morning). Jesus was right. Would YOU deny even knowing him?**

# What if ...

someone asks *you* if you are a Christian? Doodle all the places where you could tell about Jesus today. C'mon ... you go lots of places.

Dear God,
Today I'm gonna tell these peeps,
like _____, _____,
and _____, about you
(NOT deny knowing you)!!!
Amen

# TOO YOUNG. NOT!

# SERIOUSLY?
## LET ME SEE THAT!

*But the Lord said to me, "Do not say, 'I am too young.' Do not be afraid of them, for I am with you and will rescue you," declares the LORD.*

Jeremiah 1:7–8

Read more about God's call to Jeremiah in Jeremiah 1:4–19!

## Fill in some important dates on this timeline.

Before I
Was Born

Born

# What if ...

God calls you? (He's doing that, you know.) Write your age down in **BIG HUGE NUMBERS**. Then doodle all the things God is calling you to do. Today. No matter how old you are.

# 14

# SERIOUSLY?
## LET ME SEE THAT!

*I do not understand what I do. For what I want to do I do not do, but what I hate I do.*

Romans 7:15

Sometimes (or maybe often) you might wonder, *Why did I do THAT?* Sooo ... when confused ... P-R-A-Y!

# What if ...

you did something not so great? Do you think God was surprised? **yes no**

Not likely that you surprised God. He knows EVERYTHING! Think he still loves you? OF COURSE!

Got questions for God? Sometimes wonder, *Why did I do that?* Jot questions inside and around the question marks.

# 15

## SERIOUSLY?
## LET ME SEE THAT!

*They only heard the report: "The man who formerly persecuted us is now preaching the faith he once tried to destroy." And they praised God because of me.*

Galatians 1:23–24

Paul was born with the name of Saul. Saul was not a nice man. In fact, he was mean to Christians. Then Saul understood that Jesus really was the Savior. Saul changed **COMPLETELY.**

# What if ...

God looked closer. (He does that.) Would he say, "Keep on goin'" (make a straight arrow) or "You're needin' a change" (make a U-turn arrow)?

words

thoughts

attitude

actions

body language

activities

# SERIOUSLY?
## LET ME SEE THAT!

*Commit to the LORD whatever you do, and he will establish your plans.*

Proverbs 16:3

**The Lord will make it clear which way to go if you pray. Nice.**

Get an old map. Glue it around this page.

# What if ...

you commit your life to the Lord? The Bible says that he will establish (think *make right with God*) your plans. Doodle a map from your house to your school or church.

Dear God,
Thanks for being with me and guiding
my path as I _____,
_____,
and _____!
Amen

# SERIOUSLY?
## LET ME SEE THAT!

"You have heard that it was said, 'Love your neighbor and hate your enemy.' But I tell you, love your enemies and pray for those who persecute you."

Matthew 5:43–44

Jesus taught about enemies. Get 'em back? No. Never give in? No. They gotta be wrong? No. They got it coming to them? No. No. No. Jesus said that we should love others (think *try to get along*). Yep. Otherwise, aren't you just like them?

# What if . . .

you tried to make peace with peeps who are NOT your friends—you know, the make-life-difficult ones?

- ☐ Draw a pencil line down the middle of this page.

- ☐ Have a gripe with someone? Make that line darker.

- ☐ Write your idea on one side. Write his idea on the other.

- ☐ Hey! Did you make peace with him? Erase the line. Erase the ideas.

- ☐ Make a peace sign on the top, bottom, or side of this page.

- ☐ Next disagreement ... repeat.

# 18

## SERIOUSLY? LET ME SEE THAT!

*A champion named Goliath, who was from Gath, came out of the Philistine camp. His height was six cubits and a span ... Then he took his staff in his hand, chose five smooth stones from the stream, put them in the pouch of his shepherd's bag and, with his sling in his hand, approached the Philistine ... "All those gathered here will know that it is not by sword or spear that the Lord saves; for the battle is the LORD's, and he will give all of you into our hands."*

1 Samuel 17:4, 40, 47

Read all about the bully battle in 1 Samuel 17:1 – 50!

## What if ... a bully ...

called you
a name

laughed
at you

said mean
things to you

put food on
your clothes

shoved
you

Who is more powerful
than any bully dude?

# THIS IS GOD's BATTLE!

Doodle a battle

# SERIOUSLY?
## LET ME SEE THAT!

*Better a patient person than a warrior, one with self-control than one who takes a city.*

Proverbs 16:32

**Doodle a Christian you admire.
What words would you write along
the bottom to describe their character?**

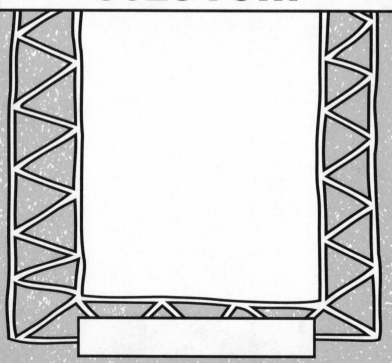

## AND THE AWARD GOES TO...

# What if ...

you doodled your character? What would you look like? Add words at the side to explain.

## Be HONEST!

The Bible teaches about character. Yep. You have one. How is it? Warrior or patient person? Self-control is better than warrior force. Just sayin' ... no ... the BIBLE is sayin'.

# 20

# SERIOUSLY?
## LET ME SEE THAT!

*Let love and faithfulness never leave you; bind them around your neck, write them on the tablet of your heart. Then you will win favor and a good name in the sight of God and man.*

*Proverbs 3:3 – 4*

Need an upgrade? (We ALL do, man!) What apps (think *habits*) would help you live more like Jesus? (Hey — look at the verses for two ideas.) Draw those apps in the boxes below.

# What if . . .

Jesus did a screen shot of your heart tablet? Be honest, dude! Doodle it here.

# SERIOUSLY?
## LET ME SEE THAT!

"I know your deeds, that you are neither cold nor hot. I wish you were either one or the other! So, because you are lukewarm—neither hot nor cold—I am about to spit you out of my mouth."

Revelation 3:15–16

## What if . . .

you took your temp? For following Jesus. Draw the thermometer here.

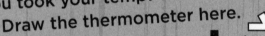

My temp?
(circle one)

cold

lukewarm

hot

God wants you to be on fire
for him. Doodle or write some
ways you could do that ...

at the top of the page

at the bottom of the page

on the side of the page

every place you see space

# 22

# SERIOUSLY?
## LET ME SEE THAT!

*I know that there is nothing better for people than to be happy and to do good while they live.*

Ecclesiastes 3:12

# What if . . .

you start smiling 'cause the all-powerful God loves you (not because your mom said to smile for a picture)? Smile. Take a pic. Glue selfie here.

Dear God,
I'm gonna try doing some more good things:

Just between us.
Amen

**RUN MAN RUN**

# SERIOUSLY?
## LET ME SEE THAT!

*You were running a good race. Who cut in on you to keep you from obeying the truth? That kind of persuasion does not come from the one who calls you.*

Galatians 5:7–8

How will your life race for God look? Find some mud. Shoe in mud. Now. Print part of your kicker here.

# What if ...

you ran boldly for God—not letting other people or things distract you? How many words can you think of that tell *HOW* you will run (follow God)? Fill up the space around your kicker. Then, wash your hands—or not.

# 24

# SERIOUSLY?
## LET ME SEE THAT!

May the God of hope fill you with all joy and peace as you trust in him, so that you may overflow with hope by the power of the Holy Spirit.

Romans 15:13

R U **STUFFED?** In a God-way, you know. That is healthy.

# STUFFED

Even better for you than veggies. (Yes. You read it right.)

# What if ...

you are stuffed in a God-way? (Hint: You overflow/are stuffed with _____ and _____.) Draw those words as big as you can make them on this page.

# 25

# SERIOUSLY?
## LET ME SEE THAT!

*And that is what happened. Gideon rose early the next day; he squeezed the fleece and wrung out the dew—a bowlful of water.*

Judges 6:38

Read ALL about it here—Judges 6.

# What if ...

God picked a sign right now to get your attention?
What would he pick? Go on. Pick all that would work.

a song

an app

a text

a TV commercial

a movie

a book

an email

a phone call

a quiet feeling

all of these

Gideon asked God for a sign. Gideon placed a fleece (think *piece of wool*) out at night. The next morning, the fleece was wet, but the area around it was dry. Actually, the next night God did just the opposite (dry fleece, wet ground). Talk about a sign!

# 26

You got things to say. Things that you wonder. Questions. Annoying things. Down things. Happy, exciting things. Things you wanna do. Did you know that the Bible says you can pray and God will listen to your prayers?

# SERIOUSLY?
## LET ME SEE THAT!

*I call on you, my God, for you will answer me; turn your ear to me and hear my prayer.*

Psalm 17:6

# SERIOUSLY?
## LET ME SEE THAT!

*"Which of these three do you think was a neighbor to the man who fell into the hands of robbers?"*

*The expert in the law replied, "The one who had mercy on him."*

*Jesus told him, "Go and do likewise."*

Luke 10:36–37

**Read the deets in Luke 10:25–37!**

## "Love your neighbor"
but who is that?
Everyone you see.

### Who are some of your neighbors?
Fill in their names here.

_ _ _ _ _

_ _ _ _        _ _ _ _ _ _

_ _ _ _ _ _        _ _ _ _ _

_ _ _ _

# What if . . .

you see someone who is in need?
Circle the choices Jesus would make.

look away

ask someone
to help

pray for that
person

share what
you have

keep going

get annoyed

pretend to
be busy

be patient

Doodle some things you might do or
give to help someone else.

# 28

# SERIOUSLY?
## LET ME SEE THAT!

*But when you give to the needy, do not let your left hand know what your right hand is doing, so that your giving may be in secret. Then your Father, who sees what is done in secret, will reward you.*

Matthew 6:3–4

**SECRET MOVES**

# What if ...

you helped others with ONE hand? Trace your left hand (on the left page) and your right hand (on the right page). Then write or doodle what each hand does to help someone today. Halt! If your left hand did something, write it down with your left hand.

# 29

# SERIOUSLY?
## LET ME SEE THAT!

That night the LORD appeared to him [Isaac] and said, "I am the God of your father Abraham. Do not be afraid, for I am with you."

Genesis 26:24

The Bible is filled with stories about God's love for families. The most wonderful thing is that God is Dad to people in the Bible and to Y-O-U!

Doodle pics of you, your dad, your grandfathers, your great-grandfathers (on the top). Wow! God promised to be with all of them and with your descendants (think your *kids and grandkids*) too!

# What if ...

you are the dad? (Someday you probably will be!) What will you tell your own kids about God?

_____

_____

_____

# 30

**SERIOUSLY?**
LET ME SEE THAT!

Since we live by the Spirit, let us keep in step with the Spirit. Let us not become conceited, provoking and envying each other.

Galatians 5:25–26

# What if ...

you tried to avoid the things listed in Galatians 5:25–26 with the Spirit's help? Doodle other NOTs in the circles below. You know — like picking a fight (okay, even just an argument) or being jealous.

Dear God,
Here is one time I let the Spirit help:

_____.

Here is one time I COULD HAVE let the Spirit help:

_____.

I'm working on it!
Amen

# 31

## SERIOUSLY? LET ME SEE THAT!

*"The Nile will teem with frogs. They will come up into your palace and your bedroom and onto your bed, into the houses of your officials and on your people, and into your ovens and kneading troughs."*

*Exodus 8:3*

Frogs were EVERYWHERE! Frogs are cool unless they are EVERYWHERE.

Read all about the plague of frogs in Exodus 8:1–15!

# What if ...

God used frogs EVERYWHERE to get your attention? Doodle 'em here and all over the page.

Okay. So what would God be trying to tell you? Jot yur thots.

Seriously. Does God need to call in frogs to get his message across?

# 32

# SERIOUSLY?
## LET ME SEE THAT!

*Do not be misled: "Bad company corrupts good character."*

1 Corinthians 15:33

COPY
THESE
WORDS

BAD COMPANY CORRUPTS GOOD CHARACTER.

HERE

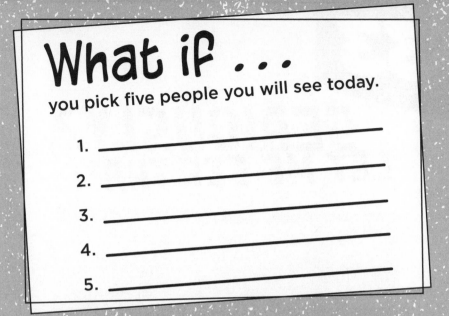

# What if . . .

you pick five people you will see today.

1. _____
2. _____
3. _____
4. _____
5. _____

The Bible teaches about those with bad behavior. Pick one from your list with AWESOME behavior. Draw his picture with heavy lines in the frame labeled "My Bud." Fold the page, so his picture covers yours. Press hard and rub the backside of the paper to copy his pic onto YOUR pic.

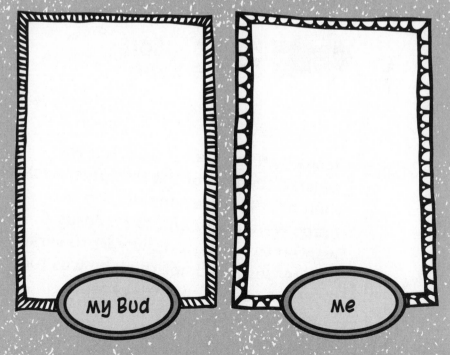

My Bud

Me

# 33

# SERIOUSLY?
## LET ME SEE THAT!

*"I have set you an example that you should do as I have done for you. Very truly I tell you, no servant is greater than his master, nor is a messenger greater than the one who sent him. Now that you know these things, you will be blessed if you do them."*

John 13:15–17

Step in some mud.

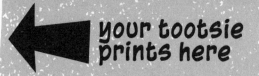

your tootsie prints here

Jesus was the Son of God, but HE washed the feet of the disciples! Back then people wore sandals, and the roads were dusty and dirty. Jesus wanted to teach his followers to serve others. Jesus did not think he was too good to wash stinkin' dirty feet.

# What if ...

you washed someone's feet? How would you feel?

- ☐ Humble, happy to do it
- ☐ Grossed out but willing
- ☐ No way! I don't even wash my own feet.

Look at the nearest person. Doodle his shoes here and how much crud is on the soles.

# 34

# SERIOUSLY?
## LET ME SEE THAT!

In the same way, you who are younger, submit yourselves to your elders. All of you, clothe yourselves with humility toward one another, because, "God opposes the proud but shows favor to the humble."

Humble yourselves, therefore, under God's mighty hand, that he may lift you up in due time.

1 Peter 5:5–6

# What if ...

you had to eat humble pie? When someone is wrong and then realizes it, they might feel a little (or a lot) embarrassed. God wants you to start out being humble. Then U don't have to be wrong or embarrassed.

## Doodle a yummy pie here.

## God's kind of humble pie

(Be humble at the start. Don't put yourself in an embarrassing situation!)

Now cut the pie. What are some areas in which you can be humble? Label each piece of the pie (sports, grades, skills, etc.)

# 35

# SERIOUSLY?
## LET ME SEE THAT!

Then Samson prayed to the LORD, "Sovereign LORD, remember me. Please, God, strengthen me just once more."

*Judges 16:28*

Samson was **STRONG**. He vowed never to cut his hair. Obeying God made Samson strong. How strong was he? Samson could push huge pillars right to the ground. Doodle that scene here.

ME —
no haircut ever

ME —
crew cut

# What if ...

you pray to God for strength? There are all kinds of strength, you know. What will you pray for? Strength to be ...

patient     wise     helpful

kind     generous     responsible

_____ (add your idea)

_____ (add your idea)

# 36

## SERIOUSLY? LET ME SEE THAT!

> Live such good lives among the pagans that, though they accuse you of doing wrong, they may see your good deeds and glorify God on the day he visits us.
>
> 1 Peter 2:12

# RULES

# What if ...
## you *really* rock the rules?

| rules I could rock (obey) | rules I have a hard time obeyin' |
|---|---|
| _____ | _____ |
| _____ | _____ |
| _____ | _____ |
| _____ | _____ |

## Who's watching you?

↓

# 37

## SERIOUSLY?
## LET ME SEE THAT!

*The people who know their God will firmly resist him [an evil king].*

Daniel 11:32

God warned Daniel about those who would attack God's people. One way? They would use pressure that would cause the people to ignore God's ways. Hmmm ... pressure. How do you handle pressure? Doodle it.

Write about what pressure would do
to the following items:

a soda bottle

your big toe

a balloon

# What if . . .

someone challenges you to do something
you know is wrong? How would you resist
the pressure?

_____

_____

_____

# 38

## SERIOUSLY?
### LET ME SEE THAT!

Then Simon Peter, who had a sword, drew it and struck the high priest's servant, cutting off his right ear ... Jesus commanded Peter, "Put your sword away! Shall I not drink the cup the Father has given me?"

John 18:10 – 11

Sometimes people make me SO MAD! Why?

# What if ...

someone attacks your faith in Jesus? How should you react?

punch
the dude

yell

deep
breath

Doodle three
ways you
handle it
Jesus' way
(no violence).

Dear God,
Today I'm gonna react your way by (doing what)
_____, _____,
and _____. Thanks for being an
example of staying cool.
Amen

# 39

# SERIOUSLY?
## LET ME SEE THAT!

*Then Joseph said to his brothers, "Come close to me." When they had done so, he said, "I am your brother Joseph, the one you sold into Egypt! And now, do not be distressed and do not be angry with yourselves for selling me here, because it was to save lives that God sent me ahead of you."*

*Genesis 45:4 – 5*

Read the deets about Joseph and his bros in Genesis 37 – 46:29! Joseph used a silver cup to get the opp to see his bros again. What could you use to get a chance to forgive someone? (Maybe clean up room to get to talk to a sib … ) **Doodle it.**

# What if ...

someone did wrong to you—big time (or even small time)?

Draw a pic of a time when someone wronged you. Then doodle symbols around it that represent God's love and forgiveness.

## 40

# SERIOUSLY?
## LET ME SEE THAT!

There the angel of the LORD appeared to him in flames of fire from within a bush. Moses saw that though the bush was on fire it did not burn up. So Moses thought, "I will go over and see this strange sight — why the bush does not burn up."...

"Do not come any closer," God said. "Take off your sandals, for the place where you are standing is holy ground."

Exodus 3:2–3, 5

# FIRE!

God got Moses' attention!

# What if ...

God is trying to get your attention? He is, you know. Circle all of the ones that God uses to speak to you.

when I see people in need

when I read my Bible

when something great happens

when I watch other Christians

when I hear teaching about God

when I pray

when something bad or sad happens

when (add your idea)

## Doodle about each sentence:

Sometimes God touches our **hearts**.

Sometimes we **see** things that remind us of God.

Sometimes God causes us to **think** about him.

Sometimes we **hear** things about God.

# 41

# SERIOUSLY?
## LET ME SEE THAT!

*And God spoke all these words: "I am the LORD your God, who brought you out of Egypt, out of the land of slavery. You shall have no other gods before me."*

Exodus 20:1–3

Draw pic of some people, groups, books, magazines, or shows that are important to you.

Put a plus sign and doodles around the ones that encourage you to spend time with God.

# What if ...

you are way more
worried about
what people say
than what the
Bible teaches?

How can you
award God first
place? Jot your
thoughts here

# 42

# SERIOUSLY?
## LET ME SEE THAT!

*But the following morning when they rose, there was Dagon, fallen on his face on the ground before the ark of the LORD! His head and hands had been broken off and were lying on the threshold; only his body remained.*

1 Samuel 5:4

**Read more about the idol that failed in 1 Samuel 5:1–4!**

The Philistines took the ark of the covenant to the temple of an idol named Dagon.

## Wrong Move!

# What if . . .

you put God's Word in front of your idols?
What idols would fail?

false idols
here

## VS.

God's Word
here

Dude! Keep score! Write down all the idols
(think *possessions*) in your life. Then write
what God's Word says about it. Score one
for God each time! Tally, man, tally.

GOD: (tally here)

idols: (tally here)

# 43

## HIS NAME

## SERIOUSLY?
## LET ME SEE THAT!

*"You shall not misuse the name of the Lord your God, for the LORD will not hold anyone guiltless who misuses his name."*

*Exodus 20:7*

Doodle your name.

# What if . . .

you are telling your bud about God? What words could describe him? Doodle those words to show more about him (think big bold letters for words like **powerful** or **mighty**).

# 44

# SERIOUSLY?
## LET ME SEE THAT!

*Six days you shall labor and do all your work, but the seventh day is a sabbath to the LORD your God.*

*Exodus 20:9–10*

What did God do on the first six days of Creation? What did he do on Day 7? Look it up in Genesis 1:1–2:3. Doodle it in the boxes here.

One day is different than the others — the day that God rested after making the world. You should rest too. Sunday. Take it off. Spend it with God.

# What if . . .

you make Sunday really different?
   How would you honor God on Sunday even
more than the other days?

## 45

# SERIOUSLY?
## LET ME SEE THAT!

"Honor your father and your mother."

*Exodus 20:12*

# RESPECT
# LISTEN TO
# OBEY

# What if . . .

you honor your parents?

Here is me
honoring my mom.

Here is me
honoring my dad.

God wants you to honor your parents. WARNING!
They are gonna love it! Hey! Every time you
honor your mom or dad today, draw a pic of their
happy face. Can you fill up the space? Maybe
you should honor them a few more times today.
Just sayin'.

# 46

# SERIOUSLY?
## LET ME SEE THAT!

*"In your anger do not sin": Do not let the sun go down while you are still angry."*

Ephesians 4:26

Mad. Sometimes you feel it. You know when. Sometimes it's people. Sometimes it's you. Y-O-U. Sometimes it's things or maybe nothing exactly.

Use colors and shapes—or even cartoon characters—to doodle how you feel when you are mad.

# What if . . .

you switched it up? Instead of mad thinkin' . . . you pray?

mad thinkin'

prayin'

That prayin' idea looks great!

## 47

# SERIOUSLY?
## LET ME SEE THAT!

*"Moses said to the people, "Do not be afraid ...
God will be with you to keep you from sinning.""*

Exodus 20:20

1-2-3-4-5-6-7-8-9-10.

**There are 10 commandments.**

## Quick, can you list them all?
(Turn to Exodus 20 for help.)

1.

2.

3.

4.

5.

6.

7.

8.

9.

10.

No prob.

# What if . . .

you need some neon paper for a project. You notice there is a lot of neon paper on the shelf in science class. What would you do?

_____

# 48

# SERIOUSLY?
## LET ME SEE THAT!

"You shall not give false testimony against your neighbor."

*Exodus 20:16*

### 5 things that are true

### 5 things that are false

# What if . . .

you kind of blamed someone else for something you did? What if you just said, "It wasn't me," when it really was? Is that lying? (The Bible calls lying giving false testimony.)

---

Doodle other ways people might lie. Then draw a **No Way** sign over each one.

# 49

## SERIOUSLY?
### LET ME SEE THAT!

*"You shall not covet your neighbor's house ...
or anything that belongs to your neighbor."*

Exodus 20:17

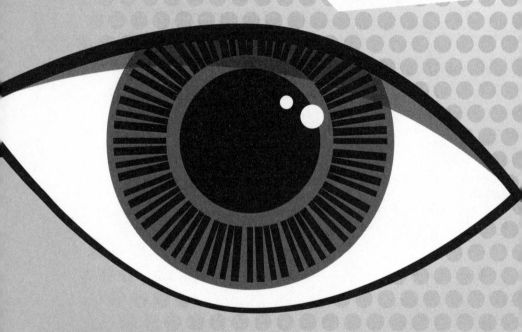

# What if ...

your friend gets a very cool game? Think of
a game that you ALWAYS wanted. He has it.
Not you.

Doodle all the ways your eyes look when you really, really wish you had someone else's stuff. Then doodle how your eyes look when you are happy for someone else. Add mouths. Don't forget the eyebrows!

Dear God,
Sometimes I am jealous of others, like when ...

_____

_____

Please help me to be happy for others, not jealous.
Amen

# 50

# SERIOUSLY?
## LET ME SEE THAT!

*"And by that will, we have been made holy through the sacrifice of the body of Jesus Christ once for all ... Then he [the Holy Spirit] adds: 'Their sins and lawless acts I will remember no more.'"*

Hebrews 10:10, 17

# What if ...

a list of your goofs was on a computer screen? When you accept Jesus, it is like he hits a giant **Delete** button of guilt from your life. Jot your goofs on the computer screen here.

Add a **Delete** button. Then draw red X's through each of your goofs. Write out thanks to Jesus.

Dear Jesus,
Thank you for ...

Amen

# 51

# SERIOUSLY?
## LET ME SEE THAT!

"Whatever you do, work at it with all your heart, as working for the LORD, not for human masters."

Colossians 3:23

Doodle one responsibility you have. How do you look when you are working for God and not just for people?

# What if ...

you make a list of things you work hard at doing? It doesn't mean you will be good at everything. It does mean that God wants you to do your best.

| I give my best effort to: | The results: |
| --- | --- |
|  |  |
|  |  |
|  |  |
|  |  |

# 52

# SERIOUSLY?
## LET ME SEE THAT!

*"When Jesus reached the spot, he looked up and said to him, 'Zacchaeus, come down immediately. I must stay at your house today.'"*

*Luke 19:5*

Read all about what happened next in Luke 19:1–10!

Jesus came to earth in the form of a man. He slept. He ate. Sometimes his eating upset people. One time, the big deal was that Jesus ate with a tax collector. Doodle what you think a tax collector might have looked like.

# What if ...

Jesus came to your place for chow? What would **you** feed the Son of God? Doodle the chow here.

# 53

# SERIOUSLY?
## LET ME SEE THAT!

*LORD our God, all this abundance that we have provided for building you a temple for your Holy Name comes from your hand, and all of it belongs to you. I know, my God, that you test the heart and are pleased with integrity. All these things I have given willingly and with honest intent. And now I have seen with joy how willingly your people who are here have given to you.*

1 Chronicles 29:16–17

**The temple deets are in 1 Chronicles 29:1–20!**

Doodle all the cool stuff that was in the temple Solomon built.

# What if . . .

you thought about all the awesome things God has given you?

Dear God,
You give me so much!

Family

(_____),

friends

(_____),

things

(_____),

food

(_____),

and opps

(_____).

I am thankful!

Amen

# 54

# GROSS OUT!

## SERIOUSLY?
### LET ME SEE THAT!

So Satan went out from the presence of the Lord and afflicted Job with painful sores from the soles of his feet to the crown of his head ...

In all this, Job did not sin in what he said.

Job 2:7, 10

Job lost everything. His family. His camels. His tents. His money ... and his health. Job had sores ALL OVER his body. Still he praised God. Read all about what happened in the book of Job!

# 55

# SERIOUSLY?
# LET ME SEE THAT!

*The commander of the LORD's army replied, "Take off your sandals, for the place where you are standing is holy." And Joshua did so.*

Joshua 5:15

Joshua was leading God's people into the Promised Land. Then God sent a messenger who gave the battle plans: March around the city for six days. On Day 7, blow the trumpets and shout. The wall crashed. Seriously.

Read all about the battle of Jericho in Joshua 5:13—6:20!

# What if ...

you were standing on holy ground right now? ANY place can be holy ground, you know. Doodle your feet. Ahem ... get your shoes off! Now doodle "the wall" or obstacle that you are facing.

**56**

# SERIOUSLY?
## LET ME SEE THAT!

YOUNG ≠ BAD

*Don't let anyone look down on you because you are young, but set an example for the believers in speech, in conduct, in love, in faith and in purity.*

1 Timothy 4:12

**Speech**
(what you say)

**Conduct**
(what you do)

# What if ...

you show that young can be awesome for God?
**Doodle it here.**

**Love**
(how you care
for others)

**Purity**
(how you follow
Jesus' teaching)

**Faith**
(your belief in God)

# 57

## SERIOUSLY?
### LET ME SEE THAT!

*For no one can lay any foundation other than the one already laid, which is Jesus Christ. If anyone builds on this foundation using gold, silver, costly stones, wood, hay or straw, their work will be shown for what it is.*

1 Corinthians 3:11–13

Here is your job: builder. Now what will you use to build? Here are your choices: gold, silver, costly stones, wood, hay, or straw. Doodle your building here.

# What if ...

you compared building materials to a way of living? Which ones would stand up for God?

| My building material | way of living for God | rating (circle one) |
|---|---|---|
| gold | | will last<br>prob not |
| silver | | will last<br>prob not |
| costly stones | | will last<br>prob not |
| wood | | will last<br>prob not |
| hay or straw | | will last<br>prob not |

# 58

# SERIOUSLY?
## LET ME SEE THAT!

He wakens me morning by morning, wakens my ear to listen like one being instructed. The Sovereign LORD has opened my ears; I have not been rebellious, I have not turned away.

Isaiah 50:4–5

Every morning.
Listen UP
to words from God.
Yes, Sir!

# What if ...

you are listenin' to God today? What is he telling you to do? Doodle it here.

Be alert to what God wants you to do today. Keep track. Each time you "hear" his nudge to do something, doodle another ear on this page.

## 59

# SERIOUSLY?
# LET ME SEE THAT!

> "Salvation is found in no one else, for there is no other name under heaven given to mankind by which we must be saved."
>
> *Acts 4:12*

# SAVIOR

# What if . . .

you made a beautiful stained-glass window to show the world the only name than can save? Draw the window here. Make it awesome.

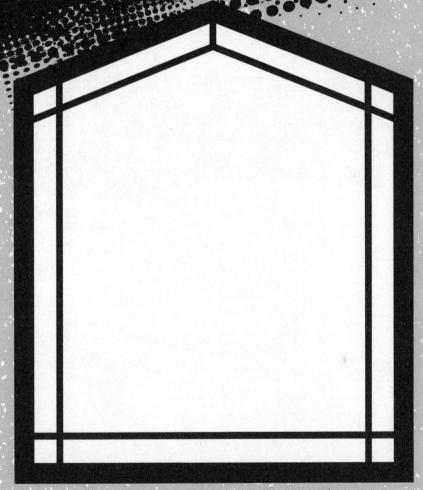

There is One Way—Jesus—to be saved.
Doodle some of his other names on this page.

# 60

# SERIOUSLY?
## LET ME SEE THAT!

Let us run with perseverance the race marked out for us, fixing our eyes on Jesus, the pioneer and perfecter of faith.

Hebrews 12:1–2

Read more about the race in Hebrews 12:1–3!

# What if . . .

you write a plan to train for a marathon? Then write a plan for the marathon of faith. Praying every day is one great idea to start. What else?

| How will I train? | YUR initials |
|---|---|
| Day 1 | |
| Day 2 | |
| Day 3 | |
| Day 4 | |
| Day 5 | |
| Day 6 | |
| Day 7 | |

What thoughts (or prayers) could help you keep your eyes on the prize of eternal life?

_____

_____

_____

_____

(This is between you, not your parents, and God.)

# 61

# SERIOUSLY?
## LET ME SEE THAT!

*Nor should there be obscenity, foolish talk or coarse joking, which are out of place, but rather thanksgiving.*

*Ephesians 5:4*

It is fun to have fun. Write your favorite jokes here. No bad jokes (think nothing inappropriate).

# What if . . .

you doodle a Jesus-approved knock-knock joke here. Don't know one? Write your own! Tell the joke to five friends.

Knock-knock

Who's There?

# 62

# SERIOUSLY?
## LET ME SEE THAT!

"His master replied, 'Well done, good and faithful servant! You have been faithful with a few things; I will put you in charge of many things. Come and share your master's happiness!'"

Matthew 25:23

Read more about gold in Matthew 25:14–30!

# What if . . .

you think of E.V.E.R.Y.T.H.I.N.G. in your life as gold? We are not talking money here. Think talents, time, friends, possessions, etc. Draw some of your riches here.

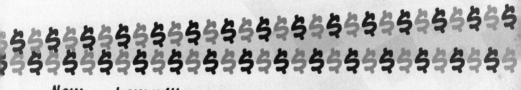

Now . . . how will you use your riches?
Doodle some ideas across these pages.

# 63

# SERIOUSLY?
## LET ME SEE THAT!

About midnight Paul and Silas were praying and singing hymns to God, and the other prisoners were listening to them. Suddenly there was such a violent earthquake that the foundations of the prison were shaken. At once all the prison doors flew open, and everyone's chains came loose.

Acts 16:25–26

### Broken. Just. Like. That.

Paul and Silas were in prison. Their crimes? Preaching the Word of God and working miracles in the name of Jesus. Doodle Paul and Silas in prison.

# What if ...

you trusted God in every situation, just like Paul and Silas? Cut some strips of paper. Make a chain. Break it. Tape or glue the two pieces here.

# 64

# SERIOUSLY?
## LET ME SEE THAT!

*Then Moses stretched out his hand over the sea, and all that night the LORD drove the sea back with a strong east wind and turned it into dry land. The waters were divided, and the Israelites went through the sea on dry ground, with a wall of water on their right and on their left.*

Exodus 14:21–22

## Read ALL about the chase scene in Exodus 14:1–31!

Doodle it here. Wind. Waves. Chase.

# What if . . .
you tried this on your own without God?

## EXPERIMENT

1. Use a large, plastic container. A rectangular one from the kitchen is stellar.

2. Fill the container with water (about ½ full).

3. Grab a toy car. Borrow one if you don't have any.

4. Now divide the water on two sides of the container to make a dry path.

5. "Drive" car across the dry path.

This experiment (circle answer):

Worked.
Perfectly.

Failed, Dude!

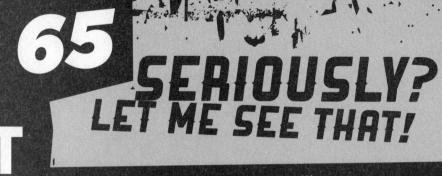

# 65

## SERIOUSLY? LET ME SEE THAT!

# TREASURE MAP

> "The kingdom of heaven is like treasure hidden in a field. When a man found it, he hid it again, and then in his joy went and sold all he had and bought that field."
>
> Matthew 13:44

# What if ...

you drew a treasure map to help a friend find God?

Directions to
## God's Treasure

# 66

## SERIOUSLY?
## LET ME SEE THAT!

My son, do not despise the LORD's discipline, and do not resent his rebuke, because the Lord disciplines those he loves, as a father the son he delights in.

Proverbs 3:11–12

# What if ...

God disciplines your heart? That means he _____ you and _____ in you. (Hint: Look in the verse.)

# The Lord delights in you as a son.

How do you feel about being God's son? Write as many feelings as you can think of on the edges of the page.

It's awesome! Right?

God's Son

# 67

# SERIOUSLY?
## LET ME SEE THAT!

Moses said to the LORD, "Pardon your servant, Lord. I have never been eloquent, neither in the past nor since you have spoken to your servant. I am slow of speech and tongue."

The LORD said to him, "Who gave human beings their mouths?..."

"I will help both of you (Moses and Aaron) speak and will teach you what to do."

*Exodus 4:10 – 11, 15*

Moses didn't think he would be good at the speeches part. He even asked if Aaron, his brother, could do the talking. God promised to give them the words. He did make mouths, you know.

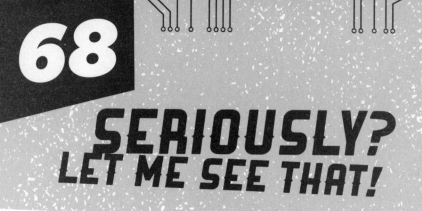

# 68

# SERIOUSLY?
## LET ME SEE THAT!

"When an impure spirit comes out of a person, it goes through arid places seeking rest and does not find it. Then it says, 'I will return to the house I left.' ... And the final condition of that person is worse than the first."

Matthew 12:43–45

People can fall back into bad habits—seriously worse than before—when they don't stick with God. Think of finally beating a level in a game and THEN somehow slipping back. **UGH.**

# What if . . .

you drew your life levels like the first screen in a video game? Which levels have you beat?

## Remember:

## your life—not a game

# 69

# SERIOUSLY?
## LET ME SEE THAT!

"Why do you look at the speck of sawdust in your brother's eye and pay no attention to the plank in your own eye? You hypocrite, first take the plank out of your own eye, and then you will see clearly to remove the speck from your brother's eye."

Matthew 7:3, 5

# What if . . .

you looked at that plank in your eye? What would be written on it? (anger, jealousy, unkindness — whatever is true)

Doodle eye here.

Glue plank (craft stick or flat twig) in eye

Dude! Glue "planks" around edge of page. Write next to them what each one represents.

# 70

# SERIOUSLY?
## LET ME SEE THAT!

*But so that we may not cause offense, go to the lake and throw out your line. Take the first fish you catch; open its mouth and you will find a four-drachma coin. Take it and give it to them for my tax and yours."*

Matthew 17:27

The tax collectors asked for money. Jesus sent Peter fishing. When he opened the mouth of the fish, there was the tax money.

Read ALL about it in Matthew 17:24–27!

# What if ...

you are serving God? Does he care about things you need? (circle one)

yes

no

Doodle some things that you might need.

Dear God,
I trust you to take care of the things that I need every day, like

_____
_____
_____.

Amen

# 71

# SERIOUSLY?
## LET ME SEE THAT!

"You are the light of the world. A town built on a hill cannot be hidden. Neither do people light a lamp and put it under a bowl. Instead they put it on its stand, and it gives light to everyone in the house. In the same way, let your light shine before others, that they may see your good deeds and glorify your Father in heaven."

Matthew 5:14–16

**Something great U did**

**Something NOT so great**

Now doodle around the one that shines for Jesus.

# What if . . .

you think about all the peeps who see you? Eyeballs are on U. What kind of light R U? Doodle a light here.

Doodle other lights for the friends or family who shine for God. Name them.

# 72

# SERIOUSLY?
## LET ME SEE THAT!

"'These wicked people, who refuse to listen to my words, who follow the stubbornness of their hearts and go after other gods to serve and worship them, will be like this belt — completely useless! For as a belt is bound around the waist, so I bound all the people of Israel and all the people of Judah to me,' declares the Lord, 'to be my people for my renown and praise and honor. But they have not listened.'"

Jeremiah 13:10 – 11

## What if . . .

God called you a belt? What kind would YOU be? Doodle it here.

## EXPERIMENT — DO try this at home!

1. Make a belt out of something old (like old jeans — ask your mom first).
2. Draw a picture of the belt (or take a picture). That is YOU with God — a great belt, ready to serve him. Awesome!
3. Put the belt outside in the yard. Leave it there for many days.
4. Draw a new picture of the belt (or take a picture). That is YOU without God. HUGE mistake!

Belt (me) with God | Belt (me) without God

# 73

# SERIOUSLY?
## LET ME SEE THAT!

*After Jesus was born in Bethlehem in Judea ... Magi from the east came to Jerusalem and asked, "Where is the one who has been born king of the Jews? We saw his star when it rose and have come to worship him."*

Matthew 2:1–2

Worship is a kind of gift. Find some leftover wrapping paper. Look for the cool stuff. Glue pieces of it on the edges of the page.

# What if ...

you gave a gift to Jesus. Doodle it.

# 74

# SERIOUSLY?
## LET ME SEE THAT!

John answered, "Anyone who has two shirts should share with the one who has none, and anyone who has food should do the same."

Luke 3:11

# What if ...

you offered something you had to someone who really needed it? Search your room. What everyday things could you share with someone else? (Uhhh ... pencils, candy, coins.) Trace them in the boxes.

## Who could you share with?

_____

_____

_____

_____

Then ... share, man!

# 75

# SERIOUSLY?
## LET ME SEE THAT!

*Shortly before dawn Jesus went out to them, walking on the lake ...*
*"Come," he [Jesus] said.*
*Then Peter got down out of the boat, walked on the water and came toward Jesus. But when he saw the wind, he was afraid and, beginning to sink, cried out, "Lord, save me!"*
*Immediately Jesus reached out his hand and caught him. "You of little faith," he said, "why did you doubt?"*

Matthew 14:25, 29 – 31

See the waves at the top of this page? Every time you do a little water walkin' (trusting Jesus) in a tough situation, doodle a foot on top of the waves. You can do it. He's got your feet!

# What if ...

you asked Jesus something really BIG? Where would your feet be? Doodle them.

in the boat?

here?

or here?

# 76

# SERIOUSLY?
## LET ME SEE THAT!

*"But God was very angry when he went, and the angle of the Lord stood in the road to oppose him ... Then the Lord opened the donkey's mouth, and it said to Balaam, 'What have I done to you to make you beat me these three times?'"*

Numbers 22:22, 28

I've got somethin' to say!

# What if ...

God talked through an animal to get your attention? What animal would it be?

God would use a talkin'

☐ skunk.

☐ ferret.

☐ tree frog.

☐ _____.

Doodle that creature.
Add the words.

# 77

# SAY IT LOUD

# SERIOUSLY?
## LET ME SEE THAT!

*"Whoever acknowledges me before others, I will also acknowledge before my Father in heaven. But whoever disowns me before others, I will disown before my Father in heaven."*

Matthew 10:32–33

**Doodle all the things that U love talkin' about.**

# What if . . .

you tell someone that you know Jesus?
What would you say?

**Who would you tell?**

_____

_____

# 78

# SERIOUSLY?
## LET ME SEE THAT!

He [King Nebuchadnezzar] said, "Look! I see four men walking around in the fire, unbound and unharmed, and the fourth looks like a son of the gods."

Daniel 3:25

So ... what happened in Daniel 3:13 – 25? Tell it here.

title here ➡

doodle it

# What if . . .

you honored God no matter the cost?
Tell about it here.

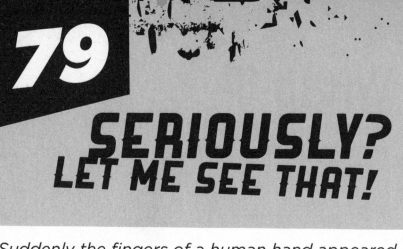

# 79

## SERIOUSLY?
### LET ME SEE THAT!

*Suddenly the fingers of a human hand appeared and wrote on the plaster of the wall, near the lampstand in the royal palace. The king watched the hand as it wrote.*

Daniel 5:5

Prediction: the king's destruction

When: that very night

Moral: Worship the living God, not gold and riches.

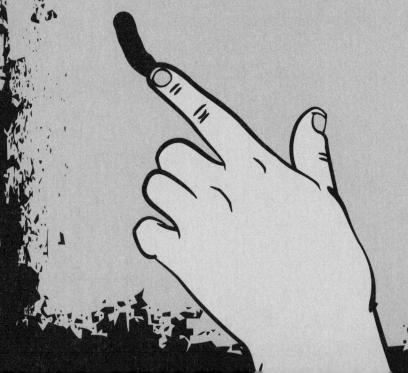

# 'What if ...

God left you a message on the wall? Got paint? Paint this space. Then write God's message with your finger in the wet paint. Let it dry.

# 80

# SERIOUSLY?
## LET ME SEE THAT!

*My God sent his angel, and he shut the mouths of the lions. They have not hurt me, because I was found innocent in his sight.*

Daniel 6:22

Read Daniel 6,
then tally the score.

| King Neb | Daniel | Wild Beasts | Angel of God |
|----------|--------|-------------|--------------|
|          |        |             |              |
|          |        |             |              |
|          |        |             |              |
|          |        |             |              |
|          |        |             |              |
|          |        |             |              |
|          |        |             |              |
|          |        |             |              |
|          |        |             |              |
|          |        |             |              |

# What if ...

you had seen the prophet Daniel get thrown into the lions' den? Doodle your face. How would it have looked?

# 81

# SERIOUSLY?
## LET ME SEE THAT!

"As I [Daniel] looked, thrones were set in place, and the Ancient of Days took his seat. His clothing was as white as snow; the hair of his head was white like wool. His throne was flaming with fire, and its wheels were all ablaze. A river of fire was flowing, coming out from before him. Thousands upon thousands attended him; ten thousand times ten thousand stood before him."

Daniel 7:9–10

# What if ....
you had that vision? Doodle it here.

# AWESOME

# 82

# SERIOUSLY?
## LET ME SEE THAT!

*For I testify that they gave as much as they were able, and even beyond their ability. Entirely on their own, they urgently pleaded with us for the privilege of sharing in this service to the Lord's people.*

2 Corinthians 8:3 – 4

The Christians in Macedonia were not rich. But they wanted to give. They gave joyfully to God's work and to those who served God, like Paul.

Read more in 2 Corinthians 8:1 – 5!

# What if...

you gave as much as you were able? What could you give? Mark all that fit.

- ○ money
- ○ clothes
- ○ time
- ○ attention
- ○ food
- ○ muscles
- ○ patience
- ○ _____ (what else?)
- ○ _____ (what else?)
- ○ _____ (what else?)

Be eager to help for God. Add a thumbprint on this page each time you catch yourself giving to others. (Use marker, pencil, juice, mud, etc. to make the print.)

# 83

# SERIOUSLY?
## LET ME SEE THAT!

He replied, "Because you have so little faith. Truly I tell you, if you have faith as small as a mustard seed, you can say to this mountain, 'Move from here to there,' and it will move. Nothing will be impossible for you."

Matthew 17:20–21

Think of something really big in your life — like a tough situation or a bad deal. Put it on the barbells below.

Write it here

and here

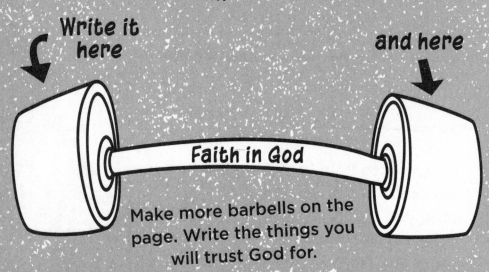

Faith in God

Make more barbells on the page. Write the things you will trust God for.

# What if ...

you could move ...?

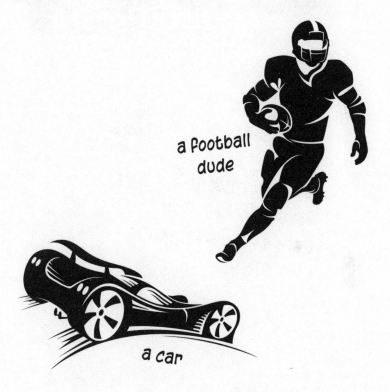

a 50-pound weight

a football dude

a car

_____

(what else?)

Faith in God is stronger than that!

# 84

# SERIOUSLY?
## LET ME SEE THAT!

*Now to the King eternal, immortal, invisible, the only God, be honor and glory for ever and ever. Amen.*

1 Timothy 1:17

God is awesome. He sent his Son to save us from our sins.

**AWESOME!**

**REALLY**

# What if . . .

you saw God face-to-face. Someday we will all see him, but what if he came to your digs like NOW? He could. Really.

Make an award for God. List all the awesome things about him.

## Certificate
## of Greatness

This award is presented to GOD for being Awesome!

_____

_____

_____

_____

_____

# 85

# SERIOUSLY?
## LET ME SEE THAT!

The LORD is in his holy temple; the LORD is on his heavenly throne. He observes everyone on earth; his eyes examine them.

Psalm 11:4

# What if ...
you think about what God sees? Doodle a pic
of what God is watching over the whole earth.

What does God
see about you?

glad he sees

wishing he
didn't see

# SERIOUSLY?
## LET ME SEE THAT!

*For there is one God and one mediator between God and mankind, the man Christ Jesus, who gave himself as a ransom for all people.*

1 Timothy 2:5–6

Doodle Angry Dude. Annoying Dude. Bragging Dude. Thinks-He's-So-Cool Dude. Difficult Dude.

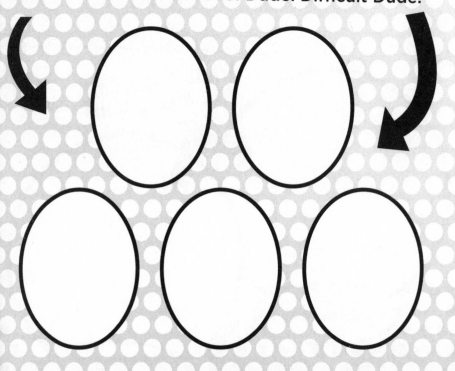

Jesus loves all people. A-L-L. **Whoa!**

# What if ...

you told Difficult Dude about Jesus? What if Difficult Dude accepted Jesus in his heart? His face would change. For real. Tell him, man. Do it!

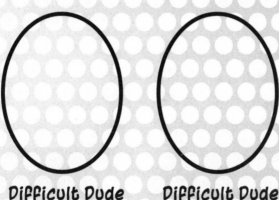

**Difficult Dude
before Jesus**

**Difficult Dude
with Jesus**

Doodle more faces that Jesus loves on this page. Stuck? Here are more ideas:

- ☐ I'm-So-Smart Dude
- ☐ Liar Dude
- ☐ Smelly Dude
- ☐ Everybody-Watch-Me Dude
- ☐ Boring Dude

Which one are you?

# 87

# SERIOUSLY?
## LET ME SEE THAT!

You are no longer a slave, but God's child; and since you are his child, God has made you also an heir.

Galatians 4:7

# What if ...

you *really think* about that?
Draw a giant X through this.

**Picture of me
as an heir**

SLAVE

When you accept Jesus in your
heart, you become a son. **ZAP!**

That fast.

Add some doodles to show that speed. Sweet!

# 88

# SERIOUSLY?
## LET ME SEE THAT!

The angel said to the women, "Do not be afraid, for I know that you are looking for Jesus, who was crucified. He is not here; he has risen, just as he said."

Matthew 28:5–6

Read more about Jesus' death and resurrection in Matthew 27:11–28:10!

If he was the Son of God, why did Jesus die? To pay for our sins. It's that complicated. We mess up. He paid for it. Scripture said that Jesus would rise from the dead after three days. And ... he did!

# What if ...

you had been the first to discover Jesus was alive again? Jot your thoughts. Doodle the empty tomb here.

Add words of celebration around the edge.

# 89

# SERIOUSLY?
## LET ME SEE THAT!

He [Jesus] said to them [the Eleven], "Go into all the world and preach the gospel to all creation."

Mark 16:15

# What if . . .

you told all of YOUR world about the gospel of Jesus?

Draw the world here. Draw where you live and all the places you go in your world—school, home, etc.

Jesus gave his disciples a mission. He said that they should go to all the world and tell the good news about him. Mark an "x" on each place in your world where you could tell others about Jesus.

**90**

HOLY GRASS STAIN

# SERIOUSLY?
## LET ME SEE THAT!

*... at the name of Jesus every knee should bow, in heaven and on earth and under the earth, and every tongue acknowledge that Jesus Christ is Lord, to the glory of God the Father.*

*Philippians 2:10 – 11*

Jesus is coming back. It will be like this. People on their knees. Everyone. People sayin' that Jesus is Lord.

## E-V-E-R-Y-O-N-E.

Read more in Philippians 2:5 – 11!

# What if ...

Jesus came back right now? Yep. Jesus could come back at any time. Your knees could be on the grass. Awesome. Your knees could be on the sidewalk. Cool. Where could your knees be? Doodle the places on this page.

Thank you for sharing your doodle talents
and your faith in Jesus with us.

# Just Sayin'

## Write 'Em, Draw 'Em, Hide 'Em in Your

*Carol McAdams Moore*

*Just Sayin'* is not your typical 90-day devotional for girls. It's an all-out open space for them to explore and learn more about themselves and their faith, using creative, wacky applications and doodle opps to teach Bible truths.